CW00505354

IN

UNDERSTAND AND BREAK FREE FROM YOUR OWN LIMITATIONS

MATTHEW BRIGHTHOUSE

TABLE OF CONTENTS

INTRODUCTION

According to Carl Jung's personality theory, the ways people perceive and act in the world can be classified according to the way we use four fundamental cognitive processes, which further classify as perception and judgement. Thinking and feeling are the two processes associated with judgement, while sensing and intuition have to do with perception. They all play their specific parts in describing personality depending on the preference to intro or extraversion. Based on this theory, the MBTI personality test is one of the most accurate out there and it has been used for decades in human resources management as well as in career orientation.

People with INFP personality type are a rare breed, as they are estimated to represent only 2% of the world's population. It is an Introverted (I) Feeling (Fe) type, who use their intuition (iN) to analyse information keeping their perception (P) in gear and their options open, constantly analysing and classifying new information and changing their minds. Due to this, the INFP can be very indecisive.

It is uncertain whether personality is genetic - or such factors as upbringing, geo-social context, etc play a part in its moulding. In either case, each person is unique, despite their personality fitting into a typology. If nothing else, the way we use these cognitive processes indicates a proneness to act in a certain way.

You've read your type description - you may not have resonated with everything in it, and that is because each trait ranges in intensity and has a different weight for every person. We'll see how that translates to real life in a bit. You can imagine every trait as an energy spectrum - which means there's a positive as well as a negative end. This means that certain traits can be beneficial as well as pull us down, keeping us from evolving. If you are to get anywhere near fulfilling your potential for a balanced life, you must fine tune these energies; with the right mindset, you can learn how to use your strengths to counterbalance and ultimately overtake your weaknesses.

The first thing to do is to become aware of the fact that you are the creator of your destiny - at every point in your life you have the right, privilege and responsibility of making choices. Realize that even this typology description (MBTI Type) doesn't tell you who you are - it may give you something to start from, yes, but it does not define who you are. It helps you identify what you can do in order to become a happier, more balanced version of yourself. Once you are aware of this, you can begin to make conscious changes. I'm not saying you will lead a 100% stress free life and that you will achieve every goal you ever set for yourself (by the way, do you feel like you need to improve your goal setting?) I'm merely implying that you can have a good life, one worth going through the hard times.

I bet that sounds outrageous to you, dear INFP - a genuine idealist usually has a hard time accepting ideas which promote imperfection. Consider for a second that it's more than most people have; if you are determined to grow, you must embrace that ideals, while nice to daydream about, will always be just that: idea(l)s. And that is totally okay. I do hope this book will help you overcome such limiting beliefs (yes, ideals are limiting -. they tend to keep you stuck in a state of inactivity and cause frustration.)

I have studied the strengths and weaknesses of the INFP personality type and, in the following pages, I will be suggesting simple techniques and practices and advice meant to help you use your best developed abilities to escape from limiting beliefs and behaviours and, ultimately, become a better version of yourself.

How does that sound? Keep reading!

CHAPTER 1.

THE FINE LINE BETWEEN STRENGTH AND WEAKNESS

Introvertedness is usually mistaken for shyness or awkwardness in social situations. In fact, it is just an indicator of where your focus is directed. Introverted Feeling, the primary set of characteristics in the INFP personality type, basically translates to your mind working by: weighing the relevance and value of things; focusing on truthfulness - assessing congruity. Ultimately, determining if something is valuable enough to be worth the hassle plays a defining role in the life of an INFP. Intuition is a tool for probing relationships - are they valuable and meaningful? Do they have depth and essence? The INFP often loses sight of what "is" while imagining what "could be".

Constantly analysing, categorizing, and assessing the worth of each thing or person they interact with, looking to past experiences and how they made you feel to identify patterns. The present is always evoking and confirming the past. Do you find yourself living in the past, and is it hard for you to be present? This habit only has one purpose: confirming previous hypotheses. It has the potential to make one reluctant to change, which usually stands in the way of evolution and growth.

And, because their expectations are always high, the INFP need to accept that development is not possible without change and that running away from error is futile. Perfection is not attainable, and one - not just the INFP - must embrace that in order to avoid useless anxiety and stress. Don't forget that to err is human (Alexander Pope).

Each emotion is quite familiar to the INFP, as it has been submitted it to your internal analysing processes a thousand times. This makes you very good at recognizing emotion in others, beyond what is being said. You're highly sensitive to body language and facial cues, constantly reading between the lines. The deeply caring INFP is interested in understanding the mechanics underlying the acts of each individual.

Careful - an INFP who has not developed strong enough boundaries might unconsciously take on too much of others' stresses. Have you ever got home after meeting a friend who was down, then you felt anxiety about your own life, even though before (you met them) you were pretty balanced? Has it ever crossed your mind that the anxiety you felt was not your own? Empathy is a great asset; however, if not controlled, it may act like an emotion sponge, continuously expanding, whose weight you carry along. Having weak interpersonal boundaries also means that you might feel responsible for the happiness of others, sometimes to the extent that you forget about pursuing your own. It's hard to be assertive or even realize that you do have needs of your own.

The quest for finding essence, while charming and useful in creative endeavours, takes its toll from the lack of patience when it comes to dealing with data or events that you don't consider meaningful. For example, you may consider the tidiness of your home irrelevant, while being ultra-cautious with your favourite book or extremely meticulous in practicing your hobby, because these latter are the things that matter to you. This is common among people who share NF traits.

When the INFP do find a cause that fits their value system, they will direct all their resources towards achieving the goals required by or relevant to that cause. INFP types are usually hard-working people who, at times, may even forget to rest, if they are involved in something that feeds their need for value. A side effect of this is the fact that, should someone criticize your work, you are likely to take that as a personal affront. How many times have you suffered because someone told you could do this or that better? Embracing criticism as a chance to improve ourselves is a way of saving precious energy and, ultimately, putting it to better use.

At the end of the day, what truly matters is to be genuine and congruent (live truthfully and in tune with inner values), while not compromising yourself. This is especially true for INFP types, who tend to appreciate authenticity more than anything. Yet, some beliefs and values are limiting in nature and bring nothing but dissatisfaction. Would you still be yourself without them? Yes!

I hear a lot of people talking about their limitations in terms of "that's just the way I'm built, I can't help it". I don't believe that is true. You can still be yourself - a better version, even, if you do the work required to fine tune your energy so that it adds value to your life instead of taking it away. You can learn to be more pragmatic, to sensibly choose when and how much to give, love yourself more while being open to criticism, and allow other people inside your world more - try and you will be surprised at how much simpler life can be. The vital energy inside you is influenced by how you choose to direct your focus - it can be either empowering or draining. The goal is to maintain a balance and not allow the needle to drop on the negative end of the spectrum. How do you do that? I invite you to practice the following exercises.

CHAPTER 2.

LEARN TO BE MORE PRAGMATIC

Pragmatism and ideals do not have to be mutually exclusive. But, the truth is the world we were born to is far from ideal. Perfection is a made-up concept. Wish and yearn as you may, reality will prove discouraging. There's nothing wrong with ideals, as long as you don't take them too seriously and turn them into expectation. I'm not saying reject anything visionary, but a little pragmatism is nothing but healthy - it's how things get done. INFPs who have yet to find a balance in this respect are likely to struggle with choosing a career that meets their expectations, both financially and ability/ preference wise.

1. Learn to differentiate reality from ideas and dreams

The enthusiasm often felt about a (new) situation is, in fact, about the expectations related to it. See the difference between what is and what could be.

To focus on what is, the first thing to do is become aware of the line that separates wish from reality. How do you do that? The next time you feel mesmerized by someone or something, ask yourself:"

what am I hoping to get for from this" and "what am I actually feeling at this very moment?".

These questions will help you see the difference between your expectations and what is actually happening. For example, if we're talking about a romantic prospect, then you may find that you hope to eventually have the love of this person, yet at the moment you just like the way they smile or the jokes they tell or that they are a good kisser; liking certain things about someone doesn't mean there's nothing to dislike about them, it may just be that you haven't discovered that part yet. Do not assume there is nothing to dislike, and keep your expectations in check.

2. "Need" vs. "Want"

Another way of developing a realistic mindset is assessing need versus desire. Do you know what the difference is, according to the dictionary, between "need" and "want"? Not fulfilling a need will have negative consequence, whereas not achieving something you want will not. INFPs, optimistic fellows, tend to think that what they want is also good for them. Careful, this is not always the case. One may think they "need" to eat cake, despite the fact that their physician clearly told them they ought to stay away from sugar. How do you tell whether you want or need something? Ask yourself if not getting it will have a negative result. Doing so in simple activities like shopping or organizing your dresser is a good way of exercising pragmatism. Many times, you will find that not doing something, or doing it differently, improves your mood -there's a certain satisfaction in knowing you've done something good for yourself.

3. Reassess your value system

INFPs are flexible in nature, as they stay open to new information; however, this is mainly used to reinforce already firm values. Despite the implication of their name, "personal values" don't necessarily add value to your life. It's the "personal" part that's responsible for this dissonance. You see, human beings are full of flaws, and these often reflect in their value system. See point 2 - sometimes, it's just the emotional connection we have to certain ideas or thoughts, wanting to believe in them. They're not necessities. Have you ever been in a situation where sticking to your values didn't end well? Do your friends say care too much about irrelevant things? I encourage you to use your flexibility and weigh the difference between what really matters to you - those things that enhance your life - and what is "junk", and of no use. Practice letting go of anything that falls in the latter category.

4. Only give what you can spare

I know you are an altruistic person, maybe at times too much so. Do you offer to help your friends a lot, even when they don't ask for it? You must realize

your resources belong to you, be they material|
(money, clothes, food, living space, etc.) or not (time,
attention, energy). Before offering to give, ask yourself
"can I really spare this?", "do I have use for it?" Be
honest - always answer these questions with utmost
sincerity.

If there are any doubts about giving, it's best to
keep that thing for yourself. Example: don't borrow
money if the date of your next salary is uncertain, even
if you have enough at the moment. INFPs do tend to
be overly altruistic, as they long to make others happy.
So, this part might sound outrageous - How can you
not offer to help? Especially if it's for a good cause!
Well, that's a question of learning how to say "no",
which I will cover in another chapter.

CHAPTER 3.

LEARN TO PRACTICE SELF-LOVE

INFP types tend to struggle with self-perception, which in turn leads to frustration and self-consciousness. You see the higher good in others, and you are capable of authentic selfless love. How about saving some of that love for yourself? If you think self-love and appreciation are despicably narcissistic, think again. There is such a thing as a healthy dose of narcissism - one that will help you overcome your insecurities. INFPs are in the habit of getting (unhealthily) attached to their friends, and their self-consciousness translates to a strong, anxiety-provoking need for validation. Do you ever feel that your worth depends on how others see you - do you long for their approval? Have you ever acted in an inauthentic way just to get it? It doesn't have to be that way. If you love yourself, you will not depend on others' approval and not take criticism to heart as much.

1. Do respectable things

What is "respectable"? Think of the person you respect most. Why do you respect them? What things did or does this person do to earn your respect? That's what you need to do in order to earn your own respect.

One of the main reasons people fail to love themselves is that they don't see their own worth. People with INFP personality are excellent at detecting the good in others. You can use this to your advantage and access their resources - specifically, of those people you respect. Practice those things. To some, it can be getting up early and not snoozing your alarm; to others, it could be telling off that rude guy at work. Allow yourself to do one respectable thing per day, for at least a week. I suggest you journal these things to keep track of them. You will know what to do when the time comes.

2. Use Body Language

Fake it 'til you make it - Yes, I am suggesting that INFP should fake something. Keep in mind, though, this is for a noble reason. You can think of it as an act of imitation, where you pretend to be super confident, even if you're on the verge of a small anxiety attack. How can this be?! We already know people adopt certain body postures depending on how they feel, and that you can tell what a person is feeling or thinking by the way they carry themselves. Yes, people can tell you're insecure. However, if you take a deep breath, straighten your back and smile, you will find that body language works both ways - not only does it express what you are feeling, but it can also alter your attitude. Did you know that if you fake a smile, you will end up smiling for real? That is the simplest and most widely known proof of this fact. Use this to your advantage in any situation where you feel uncomfortable.

Note that, as does everything else worthwhile, it takes practice. It's best to start doing it at home, see how it feels. Do some power poses in front of the mirror, and don't forget to put on a big smile. Another way to use your body to feel better is breathing through your diaphragm. This will help relieve anxiety at any moment - breathe so that you can feel your ribcage expanding. Go ahead and try it right now. There you go! Apply this any time you feel necessary.

3. Do things that you enjoy

What are the activities you are enthusiastic about? Do you feel like you dedicate enough of your time to these activities? Engaging and indulging in hobbies has been proven to reduce stress, improve mood, memory and self-esteem, and even benefit mental health patients. How do you feel after you've successfully done something you enjoy? Whether it's cooking or rollerblading - whatever your thing is, really - it will give you a confidence boost. Do this regularly and you will note the difference. I know- these days, it's hard to find the time for hobbies; moreover, the INFP would much rather spend that "spare" time either working or helping someone else. However, once you've learnt to say "no", you can reserve an hour per week for yourself, and just enjoy yourself. Does watching DYI tutorials count? Not unless you also try to do the thing in the tutorial.

Most importantly, allow yourself not to be perfect. Remember, the point is to feel good about yourself. Allow yourself this indulgence once in awhile.

CHAPTER 4.

LEARN TO OPEN UP

Opening up can be hard to accomplish for introverts in general, and even more so to someone who is self-conscious and a dreamer such as the INFP. It's easy to get lost in your own thoughts as you assess something that was said or some micro gesture that you noticed, or you might simply become shy with someone new. Many INFP feel bad about this because they would like to be able to offer more of their attention. You can leave a conversation without any frustration if you learn to open up. It will take some willpower, but in the end, you'll see that it's worth it. I recommend you try the following suggestions, and see for yourself. Some INFPs have opened up and have been hurt, and have stopped doing it altogether afterwards.

1. Put yourself in their shoes

One of the things most people with INFP personality admit to often getting lost inside their own heads and may appear like they've "drifted away" mid-conversation. Do your friends have to pull your sleeve because you seem absent while they talk to you? Whenever you have something on your mind that you're not sharing, and retreat in your thoughts, remember that every person perceives the world differently. How would you feel if your friend didn't pay attention to what you're saying? Are they silently judging you? Is your story not interesting enough? Who knows how they may perceive your hesitance? Put yourself in their shoes - use your empathy and realize that no one can know what's going on inside your head, unless you share. Once you've become aware of the message you might be sending, try the following suggestions.

2. Be honest

If you are shy, just go ahead and tell the other person. Everyone has their own awkwardness and you will be surprised at how understanding people can be if you are honest. You will find that verbalizing your shyness actually helps you cope with it. Moreover, emotion is universal and most people will be able to relate and understand. Just get it out of the way! Do this if you are uncomfortable with a certain topic being discussed; do it when you can't focus - if it's the case, do tell people you can't focus at the moment. Honesty is not only liberating, but it is a token of respect towards your interlocutor. Plus, speaking truthfully is a great part of being authentic - wouldn't you say it's worth at least giving it a try, for the sake of authenticity, if nothing else? A potential obstacle here is that you might not feel comfortable being honest, because it might come off as other than pleasant. Please refer to the chapter about self-love and remember that any awkward reaction is an indicator of that person's perception and should not reflect on you.

3. Focus on the other person

INFPs are usually shy because they feel self-conscious, which means they focus a lot on themselves and how they compare to others, what would be appropriate or not to say in a conversation so as to not hurt or offend, etc. Does this happen to you? If so, try to focus on the other person more. Look at them-really look at them, and listen actively. Ask follow up questions to keep the conversation going, and if at any point, you start to lose track, see point number two: be honest and ask questions. People will be flattered by your interest, and you will feel good about yourself - it works as a self-esteem boost for the altruistic INFP; it's also a chance to learn new things about people, as they will feel more encouraged to share.

4. Reassuring self-talk

If you find it hard to open up to people, ask yourself why this happens. Is it because you're embarrassed? Does it feel uneasy? Do you worry they might not react well? Have you been hurt in the past? Whichever your reason is, do this exercise: think for a moment that your friend, a person you respect very much, opens up to you about this anxiety? Would you tell them they are right to feel anxious and should fend off any social situation? "Be more confident" they say, but you know very well it's not that easy. Inside your head, the voices of every person who has ever offended you in some way plays over and over. Don't you think it's time you took the reins of your inner voice and replaced that negative talk with something reassuring?

"You can do it!", "There's nothing to be embarrassed about", "This will make you feel better" - these are the kind of things you need to be telling yourself. Don't allow negativity to take over, shift your internal dialogue to something more resembling of reassuring a friend. Always ask yourself: "What would I tell my best friend if they had these worries?" This exercise builds confidence, which, in turn, makes it easier for one to open up.

CHAPTER 5.
SET BOUNDARIES

INFPs are in the habit of giving more than they receive. This makes them easy to be taken advantage of and excellent candidates for toxic relationships. It is in their idealistic, peaceful nature to avoid conflict at all costs. This may leave them feeling weary and discontented and it is caused by the lack of well-defined, healthy personal boundaries. Keep in mind that no one can truly be responsible for another's well-being; you are not supposed to make others happy and they should not have the power to make you feel down. Neither is anyone else responsible for how you feel. Another consequence of not having set boundaries, to someone who is highly empathic, is that they may take on others' feelings without even realizing it. This is not an issue when you absorb good vibes, but how about sadness, anger, or anxiety? INFPs feel everything quite intensely, and it can result overwhelming. Often, they will feel others' pain as their own. The good news is that, thanks to their need to be authentic, most INFPs do eventually manage to set proper boundaries. If you are not there yet yourself, do not despair: here is some advice you can use in this endeavor:

1. Assess your own state

Whenever you meet someone who is experiencing an intense feeling or emotion, know that you are prone to undertake that emotion and make it your own. How do you avoid this? The next time you are in such a situation, make an effort to assess your own state. Ask yourself: "How am I?", "How have I been lately?", "How do I feel?" and, in opposition, "How does he/she feel?" How has he/she been?". Realizing this difference is the first step - sometimes the only thing necessary - to fend off undertaking other people's emotions. The problem here is not that you will feel negative emotions, but that you will not realize they come from outside. This is how people get trapped in toxic relationships - they can't tell where the other person begins and they end. It is easy for an empath to get "sucked" into a whirlwind of emotions, and not so easy to pull themselves out of it. So, remember to always assess your state versus the other's. It will be easier if you're the one feeling down and the other person is happier. So, try that for starters - it will train you for the next level. You might not remember to do this every time - don't worry. Even if it's after your interaction, it's still a part of developing awareness. After a while, you will know on the spot and you will be able to shake off any negative emotions.

2. Meditate

The western world has been going through a spirituality craze lately, and it's not for nothing: in these "smart" times we are living, when every day we are bombarded with information, we are more likely than ever to lose touch with ourselves. People who naturally manage to control their empathy and create boundaries usually have a well-defined sense of self. However, this is usually not true about NF personality types, because they find it harder to determine where they end and the rest of the world begins. Meditation cultivates self-awareness, which is what draws that line between the self and others; being self-aware means that you understand your personality, and where your thoughts and emotions emerge from. Meditation is an act that encourages focusing on one's current state by practicing simple breathing techniques and visualization. Do you worry you won't be able to do it properly? It's exactly this kind of limiting beliefs that stand in your way. You don't have to be a Buddhist to meditate, nor must you "clear your mind of all thoughts". Thoughts of all kinds will arise, and you should not worry this affects meditation. A practice proven to help with this is thanking your mind for sending the thought your way, and just letting it go, not dwelling on it. I recommend you meditate three to five times per week, for at least five minutes at a time.

3. We are responsible for our own feelings

Every one of the seven billion people on this planet lives in their own world. Perception is a process deeply rooted in your mind and has been programmed by your specific background. Do you know anyone whose story is identical to yours? We feel and think differently about the same things. One must understand that nobody else can really share their universe. This is both terrifying and wonderful. A high level of empathy means you can easily recognise emotion in others, and consider their general outlook on things to create a picture of what they are feeling. It doesn't have to mean feeling sorry for the other person, and, most importantly, it doesn't make one liable for fixing the issue. Furthermore, you cannot help someone who does not want to be helped - that would be a form of control. Why do I say we are responsible for our own feelings? It's because we have the power to shift negative emotions by the power of thought, body language, etc. Keep in mind that this also means that you should not blame others for how you feel, either.

4. Practice assertiveness

Do you find it hard to make your voice heard? Do you wish you could be more assertive and state your opinion regardless of what reactions it may cause? Is it frustrating to not be able to express what you think or feel in a tense situation? If so, know that this also is a sign of poor boundaries (also see point three of this chapter). Being assertive has nothing to do with being rude, and a whole lot to do with genuinely being yourself, and letting others see your true colours. It's about controlling your emotions and expressing yourself in a respectful and respectable manner. "Be assertive" is one of those things which are easier said than done, but you can learn how to do it, if you set your mind to it. Begin small - practice in relaxed settings first. You don't have to wait for a conflict situation to be assertive. For example, when asked "What should we do today?", respond by stating your preference rather than "Whatever you want to do is fine". Or, politely ask the taxi driver to switch radio stations if you're not into what's playing. You will know when the time comes. This way you will manage to "reprogram" your mind and keep composure in a tough situation, without compromising your own needs.

CHAPTER 6.
GOAL SETTING

Why is it hard for INFPs to set goals? On one hand, because they cannot decide what exactly they want to accomplish - this is an issue for most perceivers; Keeping your options open and always waiting for that one piece of information that's going to complete the puzzle, make it perfect. On the other hand, you might have set unrealistic goals in the past only to end up disappointed when you didn't reach them. INFP types tend to be creative and drawn to arts, and most NF people I've talked to share a discontent over the fact that they cannot earn a living doing what they love. Sometimes people give up their passions altogether because they seem not to fit into the "smart" goal category, namely in the "attainable" part of it. It's overwhelming to even think about at times. INFPs hate dealing with quantifiable data. If you start worrying about what is "smart", you are likely to never actually start working on reaching those goals. So, how do you do it? How do you set goals and achieve them?

1. Where do you want to go?

The first part is figuring out where you want to get. Just like on a journey, the lack of a destination will only have you wander and trapped in a state of underachievement. In turn that leads to frustration which demotivates even further. It is a vicious circle. Where do you want to be one year from now? In five or ten years? Which areas of your life would you like to improve? Is it your job, your relationships, your confidence? The answers to these questions are your goals. I'm not going to tell you to write them down and set deadlines for them (research has shown that there is power in writing things down, so that part I recommend). Since INFPs are guided by their feelings, it's important that these goals be congruent with your values. So, don't think about what you should want for yourself, what society or your family expects. Set goals that feel right to you. Otherwise, you will not be motivated to reach them.

2. Be ready to let go

Sometimes, in order to achieve something, you must give up something else. Make room for what really matters. If your objectives don't serve your need to be happy, to feel good about yourself, be ready to let them go, even if you've already invested some time and effort into them. For example, if you've been studying engineering when what you really want to be is a musician, consider leaving behind what brings you no joy. Sometimes, it's leaving a well-paying job for one that doesn't pay as well but is fulfilling. Surely, not everyone can afford to make these moves abruptly - they will take some careful planning (maybe suffering through one more year of that job, so that you can save some money).

As long as it's a worthy purpose, even the most apprehensive INFP will find motivation within. What would be worth this effort to you? What steps can you take to get there? Write them down. Then, go out in the world and do your best!

CHAPTER 7.
BE AUTHENTIC

Being authentic and true to oneself is essential for the well-being of the INFP. However, when you strive to get approval and validation from people around you, much of that originality is lost. And NF types do strive to please others in order to fit in. By doing this, they curb their creative spirit, which causes frustration and anxiety on the long term. Being What is being authentic? Is it to have a linear personality, acting the same in any given situation? Does it mean not going by any rules? Many young INFP out there think that originality is just another term for rebellion. Anyone who has not defined their self yet will struggle with doubt and dissatisfaction. Authenticity means something different to each of us, as we are all different by both design and background. It's not a men's in itself, but rather an ongoing self-discovery process, an endeavour to be the best person we possibly can without adhering to popular beliefs or temporary trends, without over or under evaluating ourselves; being aware of our own weaknesses and strengths and knowing well what and why we believe the things we do - voicing them in any situation without fear of not being accepted. It also means having healthy boundaries and embracing our uniqueness, about being honest to ourselves first and foremost. Here's a few things you can do to discover and develop your authentic self:

1.   Trust your intuition

You have been gifted with a sensitive intuition, it's a part of your personality. Trust it. I'm not saying you should never question it. It has great power, and if you do not control it, it can act against you. Nonetheless, when harnessed appropriately, is the most trustworthy authenticity-measuring tool one can have. Whenever you act in a way that doesn't speak to your principles, you feel it - there's a feeling of slowly breaking apart, a haziness in perception which lets you know that you are, in fact, lying to yourself. It's that sensation you get when you act like you know what is being talked about, or when you accept to do something you don't really want to. Have you ever experienced such a feeling? Do you ever feel beaten down after you do something, do you find yourself having thoughts like "I knew I shouldn't have done that", "I knew I should have just stayed home", or" I knew it wasn't a good idea, why did I do it?", etc.? All these are indicators of inauthentic behaviour. Notice how discontenting this sort of retrospective is. If only you had listened to your gut! It's easier to identify when it says "no" than when it says "yes", so I advise you start by listening close for those times when your intuition is trying to keep you from doing a certain thing. The best way to act is usually the first response that comes to mind, before you start running the data through the conscious language-bound thought processes.

2. Find Inner Motivation

Motivation is the drive one has for accomplishment. Inner or self-motivation is when you do something because it brings you satisfaction, stimulates your creativity and you see value in it. This motivation has love at its core. There is also external motivation - related to the expectation of reward or avoidance of punishment. It is based on fear. INFP types tend to have a lot of fear-based motivation, namely the fear of rejection or failure. If you find it hard to shake off the need to please and be liked, focus on developing inner motivation instead. What do you like doing? Visiting museums? What excuses have you found lately for not doing the things you like? Perhaps read a book or go to the theatre? Inner motivation comes from an authentic place and goes hand in hand with self-love.

3. Keep a Journal

Journaling is an excellent outlet for worries and discomfort, as well as for any intensely-lived moments. It can be any old notebook, or something you personalize with artsy INFP drawings. Keeping a log of your experiences - what happened, how you felt, how others felt about the same event. What is the point to all this, you ask? It will help you identify patterns in behaviour. Since it is in the INFP nature to include events in categories labelled according to past experience, many times you will find that it is some type of trauma that makes you worrisome about really expressing yourself.

Other times, it can be values you no longer resonate with, yet still let determine your actions (see the paragraph on value system reassessment). Furthermore, until you are ready to open up and share your worries with your friends, writing things down will bring much needed relief. Review your journal every five to ten entries and see when you acted in a way that doesn't represent who you are; notice what emotions or values triggered the inauthentic behaviour. Acknowledge that those things are keeping you from behaving in a way that would make you happy. Imagine how you would have felt, had you overcome the self-imposed barriers. Then, you will know what you should be working on - what is time to let go.

4. Practice Saying "No"

A conflict of interests arises when the authenticity-seeking INFP wants to please others. An example is jumping on the bandwagon with new ideas because they feel good, and with no regard to whether they are in tune with their own ideas. By accepting everything as it comes, we compromise our authenticity.

Learning to say no is not an easy thing, especially if you've been putting others before yourself for a long time. As long as you start small, you can work your way up to the important stuff. By this I mean that even if it's just saying no to a side of fries with your burger (even if you do want them!), it's good practice. This will teach your unconscious that it's alright to refuse things - later, you will be ready to politely decline job offers, tell yourself "no" when you're about to do something contradicting your values, etc. Say "no" twice daily for a week and see how you feel. People who have done this exercise say it made them feel more empowered and in control. They became more productive and satisfied with themselves.

CHAPTER 8.
CONCLUSION

Dear INFP,

I know that the world can seem to be an unfriendly place to a dreaming, creative spirit like yourself. Sometimes it's hard to let go, and even harder to accept that change is necessary and can be useful. If you can be open-minded about your friends' choices, you can allow your own individuality to flourish. The truth is that people are always going to judge you. Their judgement only has whatever power you give it. Everyone sees the world through unique, specific lenses - their perception is the result of their own experience. Some will be understanding and open, others will try to find flaws in everything. Who you are is your choice and it is your responsibility to let your light shine. The perceived nuances of this light and the shadows it casts you can't control. And neither should you try to. Don't be afraid to voice your opinions - most people will respect your assertiveness. Remember, if you love yourself, you won't depend on the approval of others, and you will be able to treat criticism as an opportunity to improve. The only reason people seek external validation is that they cannot fully appreciate themselves.

If you want to change the world, start with yourself. If you want the best for other people, show them how well it's going for you, and they will follow instinctively. Guide by your own example, and if someone doesn't understand, see that their road is their own and they will walk it at their own pace. You can only control your own fate. To think otherwise is to believe in magic, which is not harmful in itself, yet it will most likely cause frustration and resentment. You need to take care of yourself first, only then will you have the ability to exert positive influence.

When you don't get it right the first time (or first few times), get right back on the saddle and try again! Relax and enjoy the process, even if you're not one hundred percent satisfied with the results one hundred percent of the time. The things that you enjoy should never make you feel bad; see that they are not an end, but a means to become better and feel good about yourself. Do you paint or draw? Relish the process, the small details that bring you joy - the way the brush feels against the canvas, the colours, the inspiration; it isn't about creating a masterpiece, there is immense satisfaction in just doing something you like. Want to make your passion into a profession? Take in all feedback, good or bad, and learn from it.

Know that you are a rarity - one of the 2% INFPs on this planet. Treat this as a gift and don't waste it - the world deserves to see you and you deserve to enjoy every part of the way.

I hope that the suggestions in this book will give you something to start from in your journey to a better you!

A NOTE FROM THE AUTHOR

If you enjoyed this book, found it useful or otherwise then I'd really appreciate it if you would post a short review on Amazon. I do read all the reviews personally so that I can continually write what people are wanting. If you'd like to leave a review then please visit the link below:

https://www.amazon.com/dp/B07285RC5W

Thanks for your support!

Printed in Great Britain
by Amazon